by V.R. McKoy

Raw Earth Ink
2021

This book is a work of poetry.

Copyright 2021 by V.R. McKoy

All rights reserved. No part of this book may be reproduced or used in any manner without express written permission from the author except in the case of quotations used in a book review in which a clear link to the source of the quote and its author is required.

First paperback edition November 2021

Cover by tara caribou

ISBN 978-1-7360417-9-6 (paperback)

Published by Raw Earth Ink
PO Box 39332
Ninilchik, AK 99639
www.taracaribou.com

Table of Contents

Mania - She Who Screams 3
The Darkness We Deny 4
Beckoning 5
White Lies 7
Father, Why? 9
Night Terrors 11
Masochism 13
Barren Fields 14
Tempest 15
Judas, The Heroine 16
Thing of Beauty 19
Arrows of Artemis 21
Will-o'-the-Wisp 23
The Foundling 24
Inheritance 26
Worlds Asunder – Part I: Madness 28
Hedone - She Who Seethes 31
Lay it Bare (Lyrics) 32
Bursting 35
Insatiable 37
Morning Dew 38
Covetous Wench (Lyrics) 42
Sleep Tight 44
Heathen Rides 45
Spontaneous Combustion 48
Succubus, She 50
Fermented Orchards 52
Rejuvenation 53
Revering Aphrodite 56
Lady Maelstrom 57
Aurelia 58
Worlds Asunder – Part II: Hedonism 59
Epione - She Who Breathes 63
Spring Meadows 64
Languid Lullaby 65
Mosiac 66
There She'll Be 67
Lost at Sea 68
Dichotomy of the Self 69
Fading with Time 70
Ageless Eternity 72
Resilience 76
Dowry 77

Patchwork Dolls..79
The Counter Spell 80
Evergreen..82
Enlighten 83
Worlds Asunder – Part III: Catharsis.................84
Afterword... 87

Mania

She Who Screams

The Darkness We Deny

These are the words that go unspoken
This is the voice that does not speak
This is raw and brutal honesty
The path we rarely take
This is the sinful and the sordid
The tainted and taboo
This is all we wish to hide and avoid
And it has come to speak to you
This is your daughter's diary
The journal your son won't share
This is the note your dear friend left behind
The will your parents crafted with care
This is the letter from your lover
Your sibling's laundry list
All you thought you wanted to know
Until you got your wish
So beware before you enter
If it's the darkness that you fear
The beasts within are of our own making
You should tread lightly here

Beckoning

You
There, standing on the fringes
You're right
I see you from in here
Your fidgeting fingers
Your apprehensive curiosity
Your fearful eyes, staring
Searching
Wondering...

What's beyond the tree line?
Darkness, of a certainty
But danger?
One would assume.
Predators offering untold horrors
Drunk with ill intent

Perhaps that's why you're intoxicated now
Frozen with need to know
To see
And perhaps, to understand...

NO! To understand is to join
To empathize
To bond...

Yes, come hither, I beseech you
Lay your fears at the edge
Bow your head beneath the limbs
And step into the unknown
I'll not make a sound
Won't reach out for your touch
Guide yourself, at your own pace through this madness
For we both hold distance sacred

As well we should
The air is thick, I know
Burns like smoke, smothering
Infiltrating the lungs till they know no else
Breath slow, and deep
It gets easier as you drown
As it fills and devours you
And then simply is all there is
All you've ever known
An unexpected comfort
To succumb to that which plagues

Your eyes have now adjusted
Look around, take it all in
Fetid foliage, deafening silence
See the feral eyes, gleaming from afar
She sees you, too, as I did
Senses the electricity of your fight-or-flight
Can hear the hairs on your body crackle and rise
Feels your racing pulse as her own
You cannot run now, but there is no need
As you stare, you recognize
She is you
She is me
She is life, at its core
In its rawest, battered form
She is the result of the world outside
The former refuge from whence you came

And she will guide you through the forest
Teach you well-worn paths
Impart upon you how to survive
This journey through your dreams...

White Lies

Born a baptist, cleansed with Christ
At some point was steered methodist, soul saved twice
Loved God as taught, most fervently
Till his absence eventually dawned on me

Countless prayers I begged through tears
To rid this child of monstrous fears
But the only father that came to me
My youthful body was all he'd see

I remember feigning sleep a lot
When he'd come sniffing, breathing hot
Hide under pillow, press face so hard
I'd soon black out against the shards

Being but five and already prepared
Only booze can unlock what lurks beyond there
Decreased a bit as time would age
But never ceased or seemed assuaged

He'd paint it then in innocence
A tickle fight, just scratching an itch
But a talk with a friend at tender eleven
Lit the fire in me to create my own Heaven

For God had never answered me
Not once had he protected me
Nothing done to stop the cruel hands
Of this incestuous, lecherous pedophilic man

So, armed with new knowledge, at last I spoke up
And finally, finally, that torture stopped
No sight or contact from that day forth
But no punishment either, "not enough proof"

The system's not built for such as me, which hurts
A child, a female, an introvert
It's designed for men to lurk and hide
In Jesus' name, keep that in mind

So, it should be no wonder that I'm repulsed God's name
I gave him all of my faith, but he just never came
I laid myself bare to him, time and again
Take a wild guess what it got me then

But it's crystal clear that he heard my father's voice
When he'd sing out in praise and worship, of course
Mine would fall silent, my screams threatened with more pain
I learned not to reveal, and to take all the blame

Just a baby, I was made to be sinful and hoyden
An unclean obsession with milk-white poison
But take it I must, and bare it I did
Go to Hell with your "proof", I'll meet you there since I lived it

The most painful words now, "It's in God's hands"
"Trust in the lord" - he's just another man
To defile and betray and fail me again
To Hell with his hands and his definition of sin

He was fine with his son wreaking havoc on me
Feel my wrath, White Lie, no daughter I'll be
I found safety in darkness; I've no need of your "help"
Keep your golden gates closed, I've built faith in myself

Father, Why?

If you were the real thing
I'd implore you, please, finally explain
Why you let him touch me, again and again
It scorched me to my core
The scars are thick, yet bleeding still
And the pain both whispers and screams
But just as then, so too now
Naught but deaf ears to hear me
For you're as real as a face in the sky
As true as swine do fly
As brilliant a father as he proved to be
To create then destroy his daughter
Had I known this definition of a Little Princess
If this is what makes one an angel
I'd have forsaken him far sooner
And you along with him

You teamed up, didn't you?
He always sang your praises, and made me do the same
And woe be the day I'd resist
Or besmirch your sacred name
But it all amounted to nothing
My belief in you was never the real thing
Just a senseless, undead dream
Like the notion of you
Of your power and benevolence
To tout such traits, make such proclamations
Yet sanction atrocities such as these, and worse
To fall upon anyone, upon children, sweet babies
Then demand they give you all, in thanks, and indebted
Your throne is but dust and your words but lies
A waste of anyone's time
A misplacement of everyone's adoration

An abuse of every ounce of love spent upon you
Just like him
You're one and the same

Night Terrors

I still hear voices
Down the hall
The light's still on
I'm safe for now
I hope it doesn't
But I know it's coming
I lay still and pray
Fervently, I pray

The voices are soft
Normal and at ease
A mockery of the reality
That remains "our little secret"
Blissfully unaware
That's what I long to be
To have no idea, that it doesn't exist
Decades later, that wish remains

The voices cease
The shadow looms larger
The light is eclipsed
My meager hopes are destroyed
Yet again, my prayers go unanswered
I lie still and feign sleep
It's never worked before, but it's all I have
For just like God, you truly don't care

Can't reach the door lock
Might've tried if I could
It wouldn't have stopped you
But it might've bought time
To hide where unexpected
Escape while you were confused
Maybe scream and get some help

But first, maybe find my courage

Regardless, you'll get what you came for
That's why you're here
I feel that you're close now
And seek asylum under my pillow
At least here it's blocked out
At least here I won't see
And my body won't feel
What you're doing to me

Perhaps that's why my memory turns black at this point
Won't go any further, even now as I delve
I've not tread here for years
I fear that the most of all my blank spots
But to think - I was your princess
To me, you were My Daddy
But it was you that showed me Santa isn't real
And that the Boogey Man
Very much is.

Masochism

Love is pain
Glass and fire
Burning shards
Repulsive desire
It overtakes
Like fatal disease
An itch from within
Bloodthirsty fleas
Infinite sadness
Seething rage, seeping guilt
Loneliness and heartache
Destroys what's built
Elicits grief and fear
Yet brings enduring hope
A stubborn determination
To resist the swinging rope
Cements one's grip
To keep holding on
Teetering on edge
All's well, nothing's wrong
Stay in the fight
Ignore mortal wounds
Smile into the emptiness
Nothing else hurts so good

Barren Fields

The grass is always greener
Always. So you jump
Back and forth between both sides
Whichever appears to have the brighter hue
But in your dancing, you turn around
And again see the side you left behind
So jump again, just to see
And the song repeats again
There will come a time when the fence is gone
For your strength will fail from all your movement
And fall upon that fence you will
Crashing down all around
You'll lie there in the splinters
And when you rise and dust yourself off
You'll look again for the luckiest green
But shocked you'll be by the inevitability
Of the barren field that surrounds you
You'll spin and spin, yet again
More frantic than ever before
But still no good will come to you
For both bright emerald valleys have abandoned you
They'd had far enough of the pounding of your feet
Upon the hearts that grew them
And when nourishing water was all they asked
Their own tears they did use, as you jumped the fence again
But grass only grows when given its needs
Clovers only come to those who stay and look
So, both dried up, why bother now
Enjoy what you've wrought
Alone, with no songs

Tempest

Such winds on which your shadows bend
'Tis said they play with crueler hands
Wrenching this-a-way and that
To tear asunder all good intent

A mighty force, this thing of rage
At least until the breeze would change
Blowing fierce, then not at all
To leave us wondering, one and all

Take cover now, or flutter free
Dance as seedlings now unleashed
Dandelion's wish fulfilled
Or scattered dreams as chalice spilled

Race to capture what was lost
Grasping only motes and dust
Clouds role in, it's darkening
And gusts begin their summoning

Another storm, must brace again
We'll know not what this squall will bring
How long it stays or loud it screams
It may near be the death of me

But I have faced these foes before
These demons clawing at my door
I know them well, so let them in
They know they're home
They know they can

Judas, the Heroine

Blackened and rotten
Bruised and forgotten
As fruit unpicked from their trees
Dazed and uncertain
Of why she was hurting
She pushed up on roughened knees
The fall was unseen
To have been so mean
Surely a mistake He now sees
For He loved her true
Spared her lies, spun her truths
So unto Him she cried prayers for ease

Yet no sweet reply came
No soothing refrain
No, her pain did remain
And she knew naught but shame
To have placed faith in Him
On naught but His whim
She felt shriveled within
Oh, how foolish she'd been!
That incubus tongue
Charmed the air from her lungs
Yea, her last breath He'd wrung
She turned blue for His fun
But of course He grew bored
She was nothing but whore
So her last shreds, He tore
And left her bare upon the floor

Fool, she, to not see
To refuse to believe
Her tormentor was clear as day
Now in anger, she saw

With each inch of her raw
How the real fool had erred in His play
After all that abuse
He was sure she'd not use it
And discarded her sword where she lay
Through her tears it did shine
As they fell one last time
On the hilt as she hefted the blade

She remembered its weight
Reassured of His fate
Like a meal on her plate
Returned strength to her gait
Thus she climbed to His throne
In His heavens that shone
To come upon Him alone
Amidst barren fields He'd sown
With unfettered surprise
He read death in her eyes
His old tricks He did try
Spared her truths, spun her lies
And she let Him draw near
As His songs tinkled clear
And she swooned, gripped her spear
And with rapture, His gut she pierced

His cunning eyes did bulge
And their shine did dull
Yet she held His gaze till the end
To be sure that He knew
As His death became true
That 'twas her life for which His blood spilt
He would know as He died
That however He lied
Her truth and her strength won it all
He had failed in His game

But did rasp out her name
At Judas, the Heroine's war call

Thing of Beauty

Were I to be the begging kind
Give a damn about redemption
Might his highest lordship
In his realm of purest gold
Blinding white, shining in sun
Untarnished by the likes of me
Would welcome home a wandering lamb
Whose wool is woven from ash
Blackened and charred at tips
Obsidian roughness
Scratching at his door
If only in curiosity
To quiz him on humility
Might he then apologize
Bow, himself, in repentance
Pray to *me* for *my* forgiveness
Admit that even he can err
Fallible as the man he made
His image, in truth, grotesque
Dimmed in darkness
Ugly like me
From king to serf
Father to daughter
Tell me plainly what I already know
Show me the unseen bottom of his purse
Empty from the price I continue to pay
From his insistent indulgence
Say it, loud, in open for all
That he grossly fucked up
Over, and over
Warped an angel into a monster
Then cast me out in misplaced guilt
Cursed me to feel unwarranted shame

For crimes I never committed
Debts I never owed
Has he, in secret, been missing me?
Too late, regardless, for me to care
But I still deserve to know
'Tis the least of overdue recompense
Restitution of what he robbed
Oh, the idol I could have been
Give him a run for his wasted money
Perhaps that's why he ruined me
A paltry excuse indeed
Now for your lesson, pious one
You forget your own lectures
Of the tempestuous whispers the devil will speak
For that Morning Star offered far more warmth
Enveloped me where you abandoned
And then he stayed, always stayed
Swathed me in ebony
Gifted me fiery glow
Taught me stealth, and weaponry of tongue
Restored the power you denied me
He loved me true, so unlike you
And encouraged my explorations
Cheered my rebellion and lifted me high
To remind you of what you could've had
You never did appreciate a good thing
This thing of beauty and skill
Now look upon me in dread
Frozen in newly-mortal fear
As everything you hold sacred
Turns to dust beneath my fingers
Blows away on the bone-dry wind
Your exorbitance at last well spent
Though no atonement can your tears buy

Arrows of Artemis

I am equal parts violence and peace
I am all that is roughness and silk
I am a warrior strong though I flee for fears
I'm each note on the scale while silent I remain
My heart cries out for worlds old and new
It soars to unbound heights
As chained I remain to the ground that protects me
I am shepherdess as I am the ewe
I will take the reins as I follow you
I am every high and low
Every truth and tale
Every stage of the process
Every molecule that maketh
The thread that binds and the spindle that weaves
The fabric of life and the shears of death
The sorest of smiles and the sweetest of tears
I am mother most as child I play
I nourish all as I waste away
Feast and famine
Health and disease
The lowliest heathen and the courtliest queen
Shack or chateau, ever the quandary
I am all that is wise and all that is madness
I'll drive you mad with my clarity
I am laid at your feet, though I'll never be underfoot
I'll call to you with siren's songs, yet you'll never know the source
The pipes of the isles and the drums of the forests
The pianos of the gents and the fiddles of the folk
I am all that you see as the breath of the air
I am all that you hear as the tune of the void
I am every scent of home that you've never known
I am every strange feeling you cannot define
I'm the taste of each nectar that's foreign to your tongue

I'm every thought you deny that repeats every day
I'm the safest of your dangers
A sinner so saintly
Hang me high, swing me low
For treason worst, so all will know
Then name me martyr truest
And forever sing my praise
Either way remember me
I'll not let you forget
I am all that is immortal whilst I suffer each demise
I am every woman that has ever graced your eyes
I am every anxious moment you spend calmly and serene
I am everything and nothing, never know just what I mean
By the grace of gods I pray, understand what you can't know
I yearn to show you all, yet I fear too great the fall
I do not want this torture, yet I crave this thickening blood
So exhausted from the chase, yet I'll keep running to your shores
All that allures and repels
I long so to reveal my true self, yet I'll never expose my core
For you've the power to destroy, and I will endure when all is lost
So be my prickling needle
Till each hole is seeping red
And I'll bleed there just for you as I replenish all the land
And you'll snicker as I'm dying whilst my venom floods your veins
For you cannot prick and leave untouched
Poisoned slow, you'll die with me
And smiling I will hold you tight as we join together in peace
I achieved my goal, I won my prize
I knew you'd come to me
I knew you were the one for me

Will-o'-the-Wisp

I'll not be the lamb that would trot to your slaughter
The rosy-eyed maid you would use and leave sore
I'll not be the wee one caught in your teeth
I'd much sooner sever your blithering tongue
Leave you a eunuch to marry your lies
Beating the ground, for you're beaten now
Your own pitied victim, you poor simple fool
Choke as the air leaves your lungs whilst I sing
And dance wildly in freedom 'round your useless corpse
Yea, feed the earth so you might serve some purpose
Leave me a stain to visit again
That I might rejoice time and sweet time again
That you drank your own poison fresh from my hands
Oh, certain you were that you would taste my delights
Licking blood from my blade, in that alone you were right
Should your reeking ghost linger, find my lantern's flame
Familiar, come hither - I'll delight you again

The Foundling

If you stumbled upon me
Accidentally
In the corner of your eye
On the ground, in the dirt
In a pungent heap
Curled tight around my leaking wounds
The stench of evil lurking near
Would you think me precious
By some small measure
With my scales and scars and sinful ways
Could you see beyond the leper
To the darling underneath
Find some finesse in a freak
Would you kneel down beside me
Heedless of contagion
Cradle my face in your hands
Give my tears a chalice to fill
See my eyes through the muck
Know the love they can hold
And think, "my... how lovely"
Without artifice or strain
Would I be worth the effort
To help me to stand
Could you see my torn body
Bare and in shreds
And still find me worthy
Could I be more to you
Than a mutt or a stray
Would you take me home
Please
The nights have grown cold
I mean you no harm
With my desperate affection

It's just festered so long
It bubbles and froths
I know 'tis frightening
At times overmuch
Patience, I beg you
Let me bleed the poison out
So that I might remember
The sweet taste of life
Your elixir so pure
It could absolve this poor devil
Could restore what's been battered
Revive my lost faith
Carve out an angel
From ash and barren earth
Emerge from the nightmare
A shining masterpiece
Made fit for a Kingsman
My benevolent savior
What I'd give for such grace
Any claim on your time
I'd not cling
Remain free
Sing your praises as you soldier on
For it was you that righted the wrongs
You that transformed this lovesick demon
Into a brilliant, magnificent woman

Inheritance

Please be forewarned
I will flinch from your fingers
Even if they have never wrought pain
For there have been enough hits
From crueler hands prior
That they all offer hurt just the same

Please gift me patience
I will tremble at your nearness
With repulsion and longing combined
Even through craving
The flame you inspire
My nerves will scream "fight or flight"

Be not offended
Bile will rise high
At the whiff of tangy sweat
The scent of a man
Too long unclean
My memories will force me to wretch

Please understand
I will weep at stern voice
And obsess over every frown
It's been my upbringing
That any displeasure
Could bring everything crashing down

Please do not leave
Though I'll push you away
My intention is not to play false
I assure you I'm just
As confounded as you
Navigating our way past these walls

Don't give up on me
I will put forth my best
Though fractured and tender I be
My conditioning dictates
No man can be trusted
There is so much that's broken in me

I abhor every scar
I lament every lesion
I would feed them, each one, to the hounds
They clearly cared not
What they'd make of me
Chewed up and spit out from my wounds

All that's left, damaged goods
Wrecked from the ride
Limping with tattered breaths
I'm so sorry you've inherited
Such a foul mess
I just hope you'll not be like the rest

Worlds Asunder, Part I: Madness

"News from on high!" the goblin spies screeched
Dancing with glee on forked feet
"The Devil may care," snickered one slightly clever
Till His Lordship appeared and set them aquiver
Demanded the missive and smiled sly as he read
"She's now come of age. There's a belly to be fed."
He summoned his son from the war horses' stable
Who sauntered into the throne room as only a horseman is able
Long, languid strides from Hell-raising rides
His father chuckled low in savage delight
"Behold! Awaiting you is an angel fair."
Black eyes a'twinkle, "Is she aware?"
Guffaws in unison, then speaking somber
"Take her whilst she lies in slumber.
Their guard is down, will have no fear,
And once she'd bedded, bring her here."
The serpent held his son's eyes locked
And braced for rebuttal with one brow cocked
"So, I am to ruin her in Heaven's halls,
Then toss her to you for the remaining spoils?"
The Younger had always known the plan
Drilled into his head from boyhood to man
But never once had it all made sense
To do all the work was worth more than tuppence
"I've a want for a queen, and she will serve best.
Until that is accomplished, you will find no rest."
Freshly annoyed, "Pipe down, she will come."
And he spun on his heal to get the job done.
He saddled his night mare, her flaming hooves glowing
"We ride hard, Jezebel," and she nuzzled him, knowing
"We bring home a mistress, for my father's delight,
But at least I'll enjoy the birth of her plight."
A wry, wicked grin and a jaunty mount

They dusted more miles than a mortal could count
As further they journeyed, he grew less content
Trying to stay true to his sire's mind's bent
"What use have I, after all, for an innocent maid
Who'll simper and whine? That's his game to play.
I've no need for a milksop who'll weep from my touch.
There's lemans aplenty better suited for such..."

Hedone

She Who Seethes

Lay It Bare (Lyrics)

Would you lend me your ear
I've some things I must tell
It'll take quite a while
But I know you'll be wiser
If you'll sit for a spell
I won't try to be gentle
Won't mince words, waste your time
And I promise to listen
To your sordid tale
If you'll listen to mine

I want you in your glory
Plant my flag into you
I would rather your hands
Wander lands unrevealed
To your wondering mind
I would rather delve into your thoughts
And decipher the riddles no one knows
Oh to thoroughly learn you
Know you
As nobody else ever does

I've a woman's heart
And a young girl's dreams
And a child's boundless hoping
Blind and trusting with ease

I would rather be hard
Than my softness be torn
I would rather be cool to the touch
Than to burn from your thorns
You bleed me dry
But I find that I falter
In my newfound resolve

'Cause when you come around
It's as if I never had
Any courage at all

Babe, can you really blame me?
With what I'm so used to
And with what's put before me
What do you expect me to do
It's not so easy
No it's nowhere near simple
And I've no guarantees
Like those I demand
Just know that I'm here now
And I'll try all I can

Oh, to be close beside you
Twined so tight in your arms
Fused together forever
Is that really so wrong?

I would rather be burned by your words
Than never know of your tongue
I would rather it cut me so deep
Than feel no blade at all
Against my skin
I would rather you hurt me outright
Than feel the pain of your chosen ignorance
Oh, just slay me right here, sweet darling
Don't drag me along
Behind your wheels

Don't give me an inch to hope for
Then add miles to the road
Don't trample me slowly as you go
While pretending to stay
And keep me lonely

Oh, just tell me to leave
Tell me I have no frozen chance in hell
But don't tempt me to touch
To cling, to yearn
If you can't stand my love

Oh you angel, I need you
I can't stand it myself, just like you
Seem to seethe with desire
Nothing else feels so cold

So I lash out in anger
With my scorpion tongue
Hope for some small effect on you
Don't forget me for long

Have no fear, I won't harm you
I'll just stay as I've been
Yes I've been here for years now
Awash in your shadow
Just as I am

Hoping one day you'll see
All yours dreams real with me
And the way that I am

I would take you in any ole' state that you're in
So love, please
Take me, all that I am

Bursting

What use is a bird
That fears the freedom of flight
Comforted when caged

Crying out for help
Yet shuns the keys to release
Wings a feathered shield

Wrapped tight 'round her breast
Broken hearts find softness here
Tarnished silver shines

Cannot be let down
Or thrown hard upon cold earth
Cannot fall from grace

If wings do not spread
Far better to drown instead
Waves a welcome doom

Darling, dive right in
Drift this bitter night with me
Leave me not alone

Just keep swimming, dear
Every ocean has a shore
So the wise men say

I, fickle woman
Never know which path to take
Find the stars in you

Run me through, good sir
Seek your blade like guiding light
Set my blood aglow

Pierce my skin so blue
Make me feel alive again
Plunging into me

Soar into the sun
Blinding glimmers of the sea
Stars a welcome guide

Painless, cry for me
Wash clean my indecision
See that I'm no fool

To fly or to swim
Each its own breathless trailblaze
Against standing still

Insatiable

Carry me out into the sea
Waist deep in swirling paradise
Stand with me on liquid sands
Drown all fear of sinking
Press me to you, skin to skin
Wetter still with ocean's kiss
I'm powerless against the rush
Need so fiercely to be swept away
To ride your waves that pummel me
Crashing hard, again and again
Prayer for sin - crash into me
Envelope me in searing heat
Steam emits from our droplets made
Licking salt from shoulders bare
Intoxicating, tasting you
Find me slick beneath the surface
Secret pool to dive into
Buff my pearls with water-wrinkled palms
Shining glory made for you
Pirate all my treasures buried
Carve an X to find again
Tide is rising, don't let me go
I need your strength to reach the peak
Thrusting higher, so close, it's there
I touch the sun, and grip you tighter
Pull you with me into the blinding
Engulfed in flame, hold on for life
A slow descent in sizzling delirium
Each nerve alight with strangled breath
Eyes lock, reveal the blood still boiling
And the dam breaks again
Cannot be rebuilt

Morning Dew

Wakening sun
Smarts the eyes
Came too soon
Yet again
Feline stretch
Ancient yawn
Crackling joints
Foggy head
Shuffling feet
Face the day
Coffee brewing
Heavy sigh
Why keep going?
What's it for?
What's it worth?
Tears fall slow
Aged too soon
None too well
Lost my prime
Before it came
Feeling dull
Coffee's bitter
Knives are sharp
Eyes squeeze shut
Deep breath once
Twice, three more
Smell your scent
Bolt upright
No one's there
So alone
But thoughts of you
Enliven what's dead

Brace on the counter
Losing my mind
Visions of you
Stir my blood
Bright eyes wild
Smoldering soul
Good-natured cockiness
That look of mischief
I smirk a smile
The pall lifts
You come up close
I feel you here
The notion of you
Pressing in
Bite my lip
Warm from within
Nuzzle sweetly
Shiver darkly
Fingers move tendrils
Knees weaken
You lean into me
Blissfully trapped
Silk-spider touch
Your venom is strong
Gripping my hip
Possession, control
I'm grasping for air
Exposing my throat
Teasing with whispers
Your lips seal my wounds
Searing my skin
Branded for life
Evermore yours
Hands where they will
World-worn palms

Rough on my softness
Drawing me taut
Thighs squeezed so tight
My last defense
Damming my rivers
You laugh low at futility

Sharp hiss through clenched teeth
You find your way in
Slow, so steady
My voice low and ragged
Unintelligible
Words have no use
Only you are fulfilling
Filling me full
I quiver around you
You're panting my name
I'm renewed, again lovely
Because of your loving
Your name on my tongue
Lights flashing beneath lids
More
Please more
I want only to see you
Watch you
Feel you
Blend with you
Burn with you
Stoke me
Embers bright
Building fire
Higher
Higher
I'm climbing you
You're reaching me

So close to peak
I'm dying to fall
We shudder so hard
The stars burst and blind
I cry out with you
Echoing over seas
The waves are glorious
Sparkling beneath
They envelope as we crash

I fall to my knees
Tiles rattle my bones
My head pounding fierce
Hands are shaking
Telltale slickness
Take a breath
Stand slowly
Look around
Alone
Coffee's gone cold
Knives gone missing
Locks still in place
No sign of anyone
Dazed and unsteady
Abandon the day
Dragging feet
Ragged and raw
Stiff and sore
Sheets like cruel ice
Retreat undercover
Still wet
We've never met

My god... who are you?

Covetous Wench (Lyrics)

Why
Do you infiltrate my mind like an advancing cavalry
Sky
A fighter pilot, see my secret landing strip from miles away

I've no defense
Got no sense
Beg amends
As I give in
A little sigh
Recline
Lay supine
As we entwine

Inside my dream
Clouds
We can both take cover underneath
Now
Breathing in my ear that you need me
Wow
All these years, the dam is breaking
Aching, now I'm shaking
As you take me till I wake
Another morn

Bright
You've got me feeling like a ring held to the flame to melt me down
Tight
I squeeze my thighs to quell this fire, but its reach has me hell-bound
We're damned
This man
His plans
His hands

I arch
From sparks
My heart
My limbs apart

My fingers dance
Low
Delving ever deeper trying to find
Gold
The treasure that you are inside of me
Go
Faster as you chase me, racing
Bracing, harder pacing
As the damn breaks, I'm cascading
All alone

I remember when my vixen eyes first fell upon your face
You were sure and strong and simmering
I felt the whole world quake
Since then it's aftershock
More aftershocks
The explosion's not the end
Stay for the aftershocks
Our muscles locked
Inferno builds again

I am fulfilled
Yours
Giving all of me when you whisper
More
Pouring into me, you share this bliss
Sore
I'm raw from all the rubbing, loving
Every painful moment
Wash it clean, until we meet again
When slumber brings you home

Sleep Tight

Flames aglow on glistening skin
Her siren's call rings clear again
Drawing rain from thunderous skies
Lacing through the storming night
Fingertips trail twinkling stars
On nimble limbs with moonlit scars
Stepping lithe from raucous downpour
Once more comes to play the whore
Tried to keep her at arm's length
She knows best her aching strength
Meant to slay the beast last time
But she reigned supreme as you entwined
Slay the heretic! Burn the witch!
Laughing eyes, she knows you itch
Claws sink in to scratch, enclose
Bound again to Lilith's ghost
Lick your throat to steal your voice
Knowing you don't want a choice
Her moistened lips will take your air
Snaking fingers through your hair
Gripping firmly, pull you back
Your doom rests in her eyes so black
You'll rise to occasion upon command
Thick and molten in her hands
She'll mount you sure for a swift ride
To Hell where your true love abides
Don't fear what comes in the dark to play
For like all moments, this one won't stay
She'll leave you sighing when she's done
Receding, screaming at rising sun
Rescued from sweet reverie
You'll rasp for breath as you flail free
But never forget lest you be surprised
When she returns behind sleeping eyes

Heathen Rides

You come upon me again
Mayhem in your eyes
Smoldering
You mean to suffer me slowly
Familiar throb
I know this pain
Snaking up from dank cavern
Smoke will close around me
Burn my throat with your cinders
Breathing forgotten at your fingers' behest
Squeezing life from this one undeserving
Hair gripped tight so scalp would sting
Pulled abruptly
You'll have me where you want me
Cheeks stained pink
Angry red
You're taunting me
You want me mad
Unsure what's worse
To fight or play dead
Either way your ire alights
And you plume further with fever
Place the flame upon my face
Your palm a cruel certainty
Again, and again
The blows will come
Feel numbness forming
My eye swells shut
Peripheral is black
No response worth the effort
And feel your ardor begin to retreat
I'm well aware of my uselessness
But you remind me, to be sure

Then strange, a new sensation blooms
As if injected with hellfire
It spreads through me like liquid courage
You came to play? Let's play.
I rise and meet you face to face
You see right past your recent work
But can't escape my crimson eyes
And find you now can't move
I brush your cheek where mine does hurt
Leave charring flesh along the way
Your helpless tears fall and singe
And I lay you back to have my way
The unexpected turn of fear
My wicked reciprocity
Would surely have you running scared
Were you not trapped beneath me
Whimpering, writhing, untamed horse
Skittish now when facing me
I grin and lick with forked tongue
And mount my well-earned steed
Drink your screams in as you sear
Rocking slow lest you forget
I am now the master here
And my demons wish to play
Diminish yours they surely shall
You underestimated your enemy
Now feel my spurs at quickened pace
This journey's far from over
I ride like wild
Racing to freedom
Coaxing your breath into my wrenching hands
You start to fade, and I find release
Cry out in earnest, the conqueror
Arching back, taut and heaving
Galloping bareback till slick in the saddle

My garnet flames then cool to violet
Glowing keenly at victory, peering down
I see the life has left your eyes
Your soul's been tallied in the black halls below
And I weep in cleansing, the lilac now blue
Climax again, full, on my own
My heathen road to sovereignty

Spontaneous Combustion

Cinders collapse in the ravaged forest
Embers barely alive with spent ardor
A dimly lit ballroom at best
Her steps fall haltingly
Splinters in her soles
But heedless is she, in the face of such destruction
Her tears ooze like boiling sap
Rivulets on her singed cheeks
Surveying the carnage
She'd not meant all of this
Search for any sign
Any movement
Bone fragments
If only she'd held it in
Her love was anarchy
He could never have known, when he paid her kind word
That she could turn single coin into fortune
That his receptiveness made fecund her rocky soil
That his sweetness quenched a desperate thirst
That his own tempered passion stoked her aching flames
And she conjured his whispers to swirl with her own
In a heat storm so fierce
Her frozen soul begged relentlessly
For a chance to melt and burn bright
Thus, opening her arms and her hurricane heart
She gave birth to this dangerous creature
And allowed Pandora to play
But the lecherous witch
Spun a cyclone of flames
And rode hard straight for him
To engorge his curiosity
He'd not meant all of this
Tried to flee from the ambush

But she surged rapid-fire to ensnare a new treasure
A hunter's sharp aim
Her chest overfull with hideous things
Just one wink of beauty to claim as her own
He recoiled from the crone
Sought the clean breath of freedom a world away
And left the harpy bereft of jewels
Scorned and indignant, she sputtered and left him likewise
And the plumes of her smoke rose from their bed of ash
Fresh morning dawned on the wasteland she'd wrought
Leaving her barer to continue the quest
As in centuries passed, eyes scouring and scorched
Leaving prints of charred flesh along her path
Pulling and sticking with foul perfume
A small penance to the knight she'd driven away
Forever looking to find him again
If only to implore him
I pray, dear one, forgive me

Succubus, She

Head on my hands
Chin bruising knuckles
Eyes boring holes
Into the emptiness of the glass
Like a window hinting possibilities
Which lovely lass you be?
Amber, Crystal, or Ruby, love?
Bejeweled in delicious decadence
What longing it is
To remember your chill on my lips
And the sting of your waves
The rush of heat as you penetrate
And soak me full through
Yea, I know well the anticipation
The dizzy delight
The ardent abandon
Dancing to your song
A beguiling witch
Ever youthful though ancient
And the spell you weave about me
All my wounds would seem long healed
I'm not drowning, merely floating
I'm not bleeding, blackness leaving
Those tears are just moon beams
To lead me to dreamland
What a sexy mistress you are
Ever tempting, a siren's call
But I must resist
I must!
For one sip and I'm immersed
And I'd die to dive into a wench like you
Envelope me in your silken tendrils
Twine 'round me softly, fill my throat like your cups

Make the horrors around me blur and fade
So I sway with illustrious abandon
No, no witch!
Be gone, sweet temptation!
Damn you that I can't look away!
Face on counter
Cheek upon granite
I stare on, unseeing
As the tumbler's taunts whisper on

Fermented Orchards

Skin peels back from gritty eyes
Smarting and bitter from blinding dawn
Rising slow, the cart upsets
The fruit rots black like severed roots
Escape to last night's tangy delights
Sweet as pie, ripe with gaiety
Rosy and supple, juices dripping
But sun will always shrivel and brown
Meet me again beneath the boughs
At fireside to dance and sway
Bake me golden, caramel
Love-drunk on hard cider
Remember me in tiers of red
Emerald and amber flashing
Splice me open, discard my rough core
Plant your seeds in measured rows
Keep my apple in your eye
A softened splinter renders no pain
Should I grow there for years to come
The worms might leave me be

Rejuvenation

Another uncouth day winds down
I'm worn and weather-beaten
Long to soften that which withers
Sink into cleansing waters
To find a hint of long-lost beauty
Open wide, flooding in
Renew my mouth for bolder flavor
Capture your facets on starving tongue
You couldn't know how you sustain me
Appetite for transparency
You're all you claim to be
No lies abide where there is you
You practice all that you would preach
No greater aphrodisiac
Than safety and trust most proven
Your only surprise is how you love me
Amazed at your ardor, the power you gift me
Feel the heat of your palm
Through terry cloth cover
Move it aside, skimming so slow
I harden for you, hard on me
I blush in places, pretty in pink
Darkening to dangerous mauve
Overflowing, catch me spilling
Quest to find my tingling
I'm begging you
Delve to feel me humming
Tantalize and quiver me
On edge of death, anticipating
Hanging on cruel hook for you
Don't leave me out to dry
Suckling the steam drops
Gathered in worship on your skin

My knees grow weak beneath me
Lift me up to level with you
So eyes needn't travel
Back against wall
Meet me in the middle
I'll push forth to meet you
Silken splendor
Lose yourself inside me
I'll find you in the fog
Hear my labored breathing
Like a song named after you
Match my fevered pitch
I'm molten in your gentle hands
A new sensation, exhilarating
I needn't feel pain for your pleasure to peak
I revel in your reverence of me
Pull me firm against you
Fill me to hilt
No light escapes
Trapped beneath my eyelids
In the prisms you send flashing there
I'm rising, crying
Searing, soaring
Come with me
But then it's over
Never over, won't let you go
I can't, I can't
Not yet, so wet
It's coming, I'm coming
I'm dying, I...
Oh... you are exalted
Godly, you've saved me
Reach out to hold you close in praise
Only clouds envelope me
But I still feel you, fused below

Venture to find you, slick with truth
Pearlescent proof that dreams are real
This muted throbbing is not for nothing
No other yet so brave in rebellion
To bring his full truth in rawest form
To table for us both to feast
These riches I will never forsake
I'll not begrudge your need for air
My freedom loves me too
Come home when you are ready and wanting
I will be here still
Revitalized to face the morning

Revering Aphrodite

What wouldn't I give to lose myself in you
To dive head first between trembling legs
Muffle the world with thighs squeezed to my ears
No better way to drown, I care not for breathing
The sound of your breath is too good to miss
Frayed and delicate as I love you my best
I drink from your fountain of youth to survive
So sweet is your honey, your nails pleasing sting
As they grip my hair and you thrust to meet me
My lips press to yours in bold reassurance
I taste your abandon, my tongue is your lifeline
Reach 'round, hug your hips, bucking wildly in fever
Questing higher for dusky peaks
You grab my hand to you and we both hold on tight
I'm frenzied now, on the verge myself
Till you sing out, so glorious, and I arrive with you
To that steaming paradise with unceasing waves
Where we drift wordlessly, fingers and hearts entwined

Lady Maelstrom

Sparks alight like a date with the devil
Winking at night's bloom
My pulse rolling thunder, then
FLASH!
She ignites me fierce where I stand
And never more than before, I surrender my soul
Unrepentant in her volatile splendor
She cradles my ashes to cleanse in her rains
Her swollen clouds tenderly bruise
My smiling cheeks as I bury me there
To conquer the raging storm
Soaked full through as she pours over me
Lean back to catch crystal clear drops on my tongue
Slide down my throat like chilling fire
I find myself renewed
And she, there, in her raw glory
Quelled as surely as she sprang upon me
Lulled into sleep, we are one by the morn
No longer fearing a sinister squall

Aurelia

Blinking
They don't realize what they're seeing
Twinkling
You're my kaleidoscope queen

Sprinkling shimmers on my darkest parts
Sweeping up my shattered heart
Crystal prisms, shining rainbows
So sharp I'm torn apart

And born again
Remade in ways I could only imagine
I'm dreaming of a sea where you're my captain
Sailing ships with me
Weathering the storms with me
Navigating stars with me
Igniting molten flames between the sheets

But it's your soul, your voice, your verse that holds me captive
Cannot breathe without your breath of fresh air
Need your tempest winds in my hair
Fingers brushing light-trails
On my skin, thrilled by your dragging nails
Wish I could wear your dragon scales
An armor none could pierce

I'm smitten with catastrophe
Destroy me, Lady Lovely

My heart is skipping beats like stones
Sinking in like setting suns

What other fate there be
But amber eyes like never seen

Worlds Asunder, Part II: Hedonism

Golden gates gleamed ahead as the third moon rose
Dismounted at distance, horse blended to shadows
"She had better be worth having traveled so far."
Dissolving to vapor, he slipped through the bars
He mapped the great fortress as the sorcerer sees
And drifted in through her window on sulfuric breeze
Regrouped in the corner, his dead heart beat fast
As he gazed upon the intended bride at last
None of his training prepared him for this
The softest of lips that begged to be kissed
Lashes like feathers on sleep-flushed cheeks
Lush, silken locks in a pillowed heap
Limbs as lithe as willow whips
His hands burned to graze her breasts and hips
He felt himself swell as she stirred and woke
He poised for the pounce, anticipating first stroke
But her eyelids snapped open, and she held him spellbound
Cerulean pools pinned his feet to the ground
She assessed him full measure, and he was glad to oblige
Could feel her gaze scorch him as she took in his size
Garbed in obsidian, scented with death
He was beautiful, menacing, stealing her breath
His height most imposing, his muscles taut cords
His eyes black abyss... she wanted to fall more
She must rise, summon help! But he moved like a mist
And pinned her in place by her delicate wrists

He expected bright tears and a meek beggar's cry
But instead, "I'll not fight you. I just need to know why."
Stunned, he leaned back and locked orbs with his victim
And saw truth, no guile, and was utterly smitten
"I've been sent to break you in as the Netherlord's queen."
The tears gathered there, but stayed put in their sheen

She swallowed his candor and nodded assent
And he fought like a madman not to repent
"Why are you willing? He'll not treat you kindly.
He sent me to force you if you wouldn't go blindly."
She smiled small and sad, and splintered his heart
"He can't really have me if I'm broken apart."
And the thought of her broken, bleeding and raw
Sent a shockwave through him too quick to withdraw
"If he wants this done, he must do it himself."
He released his grip, but she grabbed him and held
Now he saw fear, and her voice wavered hoarsely
"I'd rather you. Please. Don't condemn me thusly.
You're fearsome, for true; I might not survive.
But I'd rather die by your hands, than feel his while still alive."
Still not quite sure, she held his torn gaze
Drew his hand to her breast in a velvet haze
He saw her true welcome, a new warmth never known
And drew her close to him firmly, his sword fully honed
Laid her down where she'd been, and she opened for him
His clothing a vague memory in light of her skin
She was made of The Light, singed where they met
Her breaths came out ragged. "We've not finished yet."

A sweet teasing smile she'd not expected
Disarmed her, and she gave it back, reflected
He brushed a stray tendril out of his way
Pressed hot lips to soft flesh, no words left to say
She gasped at his touch, his palms wandered down
And she peaked as his fingertips circled around
The weight of her there was just right for his hands
He filled further to know she'd known no other man
Pressing into her surely, his mind was a'swirl
As their shorthairs entwined to make intimate curls
He took one last look to be sure of her heart
She smiled once again and her legs slowly parted

And by God, though that word brought sharp pain to his head,
He had never known pleasure like this, even dead
No temptress he'd tasted in Hell could compare
To this lovely, sweet goddess who held him ensnared
She tensed, sore at first, and questioned her fate
So he moved with great care till the pain left her face
Then he rode with abandon, and she met every thrust
Needing to feel some illusion of trust
She'd never felt fevered and frenzied this way
She'd happily die if this be her last day
Approaching crescendo, her bright eyes met black
He knew in this moment he'd never turn back
Their lids fell from momentum, and her voice rang the stars
She tightened fiercely around him, branding new scars
In a rush he slammed harder to fill her completely
And she quaked to contain him, "please no, don't leave me!"
"Never, love, never!" then his shouts echoed hers
Guttural growls as no one has heard
As they drifted back down, muscles aflutter
They savored each aftershock, deliciously shuddered...

Epione

She Who Breathes

Spring Meadows

I can hear you breathing from miles away
Feel it on my face through the fog and haze
It creeps upon me stealthily
So that I can keep dreaming
Of the love we shared beside the waters streaming
Trace patterns in the dewdrops on my skin
In the wood around the bend
In the land long lost within
You're soft against my mind
So hard to get to
I smelled the rain coming
Yet still we lingered on
The luting of the lark's song
The rustling of the grass
Became our tune to which we played the day
The morning so blessed when the night began
Your whispers in my ear send me soaring into skies
You're painting precious clouds
A feather's touch as I fly
Yes, breathe fierce into me
Faster
Deeper
It is your essence I need
You must fuse with me
We must drift as one
Mist on the breeze
Disappearing into our own
Never to return to the pain
Of the loneliness we once knew

Languid Lullaby

I feel you reaching out to me
Wish on silver, cast to the clouds
Rippled moonbeams lap at my shore
A rebel breath to flutter my hair
And chill me with wicked warmth
Strum a plaintiff melody
To lull me into peace
The rhythm slow, a lazy drawl
Simmering from my center
Play your song, flood my core
Melt and blend in fine refrain
Tuned with righteous purity
The loveliest of sins
Run me through with strength of word
Lyrics meant to pierce the heart
That, daring, whispers name to heaven
A constellation of finger tips
Dancing lightly over me
Imagined touch transcending skies
I pool and shudder from this dream
Begging not to wake
With shivered thighs and crested peaks
Aching across distance
Swathed in starlight
Though years of pain would thwart us still
I pray you feel me in kind

Mosaic

Shower me clean with your luminous touch
Sprinkle me with your star dust that brings me such peace
Lend me your light that my darkness might falter
And shine me to silver that I might then be worthy
Transform my bruised hues to life-giving green
With your sweet golden soul, gift me chartreuse sheen
Make my spilt blood glow as bold as the sun
So it might not be leaking for nothing at all
Bring calm with lavender in your feathered hair
My fingers have pruned awaiting your silk
Break upon me with your limitless beauty
Soften my shards as they fall and blend
Fit close and sure to my broken soul
The pieces of you will make whole what needs healing
And though I could never aspire to such grace
Cannot fathom to reach you but for your benevolence
We've puzzled together a remarkable treasure
A mosaic of sinner and saint
For there is no finer art than a woman

There She'll Be

And she will come, garbed in the night
Wrapped in darkness with the shimmer of the moon
Pale in her splendor
Silent in her steps
To softly wash upon you
Like a balm you needed unawares
And she will lead you to peace and slumber
Take your cares from your shoulders that you may find rest
For she knows every soul can only bare so much
But she'll not singe your face with the heat of her own strength
She'll not leave you cold upon her own whim
For she bares her own scars, tends her own wounds
So there she will stay
To assist you with yours
And when the twilight would come to sap her power
To send her trudging to her bed
She will chase her own dreams in her own good time
As they soar ever higher after yours have been caught
Her shine will fade and her nightshade deepen
And you'll once more fear the cruel world
But close she'll remain and in time rise again
On the frontlines of your battles
Sure and true, there she'll be

Lost at Sea

Plunge me deep into darker seas
That I may meet you in my dreams
And hear sweet words I've longed you'd say
To stave away the assaulting grey
Blind me with color as I die
Drowning in your starless sky
Beneath the waves I'll float with you
A faithful raft upon the blue
And holding hands you'll lead me on
Toward the heavens long since gone
Lost in the horizon we shall become
Two halves resewn and finally one
I've missed you so, my lifeline dear
I'd thought you'd never again be near
Yet blessed I am, you've returned to me
And I'll brave the storms to remain with thee
Love held true through lives and years
Transcended time despite my tears
In my own hell I abandoned you
Was thusly punished to search for you
And just as I had lost all hope
You appeared with hands to pull me up
And I'll never forget that touch, those eyes
Unchanged from long ago, undaunted by time
You've tried to save me from the start
But I couldn't escape my broken heart
Was blinded by my own regrets
Consumed upon the parapet
So I jumped and dove into the sea
To cleanse and rebirth a better me
To be worthy of you, deserving your love
And ever gracious, you lead me back to home's cove

Dichotomy of the Self

Blooming and withered
Unwavering and torn
Enlightened and oblivious
Hopeful and forlorn

At home amid the lost
Inert amid rough seas
Ever-searching for salves to comfort the pain
To silence the sirens' screams

A captain with no direction
Emblazoned in murky fog
Navigating the stars that lead nowhere but here
Adrift while chained to the docks

Tunneling under the heights
Of the lows that make me fly
Perhaps one day I'll find solid ground
To float me towards the skies

Fading with Time

Another sunset on the shore
It soothed her soul on days like this
The earth's light crashing to the ocean floor
To cleanse and drown the aches within

She feasted eyes on victories gained
The life she'd always wanted, she'd won
The smooth drumming of waves on sand
'Twas everyday her lullaby sung

The silent stillness within her walls
No bodies about to burden her
The telephone held no missed calls
Collected dust upon the ringer

No questions, demands, nor opinions uninvited
No news alerts - there's nothing new
No cause to mourn or rejoice delighted
Each day the same - nothing new

"This calls for a toast, this achievement of mine,
For it is all of my own making."
So she swallowed the last of the good stuff, divine
And set the empty bottle down, slightly shaking

"I'm not what I used to be, it would seem.
Age is upon me, heavy with the past."
She climbed the stairs slowly with her fogging thoughts
And sought to slumber at last

Her bed warm and waiting, all for herself
She gazed out the window once more
And pondered the waves that would take her away
To meet the sun upon the floor

Then she slid beneath the sheets with the last of her strength
Her wits a goodbye on the wind
And she whispered "I'm sorry for all I've become.
May they welcome me home
After this moment ends."

Ageless Eternity

Morning rays peeked through curtains drawn
She fluttered open beside her love
A whispered touch to tender cheek
He shivered, she smiled
And quested beneath
Reached to give him loving squeeze
He wouldn't wake, she knew him well
Rising after, she donned her robe
Drifted downstairs with silent steps
Got the coffee maker ready for him
Shook her head, rolled her eyes grinning
He always forgot to rinse the filter
She heard him stirring, her darling love
Put his wallet and keys next to his thermos
And strolled out to the garden
To dip her icy hands in the sun...

He stared at the ceiling
Hand resting where she'd been
She'd been gone for a while now
Still not used to the cold
He'd taken to keeping the heat above normal
Yet always found himself chilled in wee hours
Felt moisture below
Guess he'd dreamed of her again
She'd always made him feel younger
He shook his head and changed the sheets
Dressed mechanically and sauntered downstairs
He felt his age again
His memory must be on its way out
He never remembered rinsing the filter
Maybe her habits had finally rubbed off on him
Looking 'round the room for her longingly

She'd be proud to see he'd prepared for the day
No time for lonely reveries, though
Off to lose himself in mindless work
He turned to go, but in corner of eye
Strange
He'd left the back door unlocked
He never went out there anymore
Another chill
She'd always loved the sun...

She didn't remember closing the door
Even locked herself out, silly goose
Good thing we still keep a key under the mat
At least she could pass these dusty years with him
Tracing designs in their salt and pepper
Shake it off, back inside for the daily chores
She tidied up their little home
He'd grown more cluttered of late
Gave her sense of purpose, though
He'd be home soon
She felt his warmth nearing
She filled his snifter, bourbon neat
And chose a pungent, thick cigar
Crinkled her nose, but they gave him comfort
He seemed to get cold more easily now
Back in the cabinet, no
Leave the bottle
He may have had another long day
He worked so hard, perhaps too much
His ethics were iron
He made her so proud
Heard keys in the lock
Went upstairs to change...

His footsteps echoed heavy through the empty room
Time to get more rugs, he thought sourly

What the devil?
When had he cleaned?
Every day seemed to bring him closer to madness
Everything looked just the way she had left it
He must be preserving the life they shared
Never realized how he treasured so many little things
Till he was left on his own to remember them
His head pounding fierce, he slumped deep in his chair
Good thing he kept the bottle on the table
He damn sure wasn't going anywhere now
It was time to cleanse his wounds
Emptied the glass in a single shot
The second one came a hair slower
Then he settled in to the languid third
And in fuzzy haze
Imagined small feet padding near
The hairs on his neck rose with familiarity
Damn it to hell, even through liquor
But his legs were leaden so he downed a fourth
Content to pass out, or freeze in the night...

She watched him close his weary eyes
And mourned the shadows that deepened the lines
Sweet man in drunken stupor whispering
"I'm missing you now. Can you hear me?"
Her tears froze firm to bluish cheeks
And she reached to cup his face
He sucked in a sharp breath at the sobering cold
But limbs were too heavy to investigate
"I'm still here, my love."
He heard her quiet voice
And it burned behind her fingers' trails
He saw her now with bleary wanting
Like frosted windows encasing flame
She wore his favorite negligee

He'd always loved her skin in silk
He mustered the strength to beckon her forth
"I need you. Take me home."
And she gladly obliged
Washed over him like winter's ocean
Felt himself freeze from the inside out
She gripped him entirely
And he sank deep within her
Holding on till they formed a great glacier of sadness
His breaths came stunted
Harsh clouds in the air
"I never could leave you."
One last smile
"Never do."
She inhaled the last drops of the clouds from his lips
And passion spent, time run out, he went still

Cold on his own now, she licked the rim of the snifter
To taste the last of his heat
Then climbing the stairs, passed the hall in the dark
Where her own useless body still swung slow in her breeze
A wry smile, "Foolish lamb," moving on
Found her place in their bed
And sighed with relief at the sight of him there
He'd met her so swiftly, so handsome in ether
They entwined, and dispersed
Finally free to be as one

Resilience

As the wind breathes lightly through sheltering trees
And tears fall from the eyes of a slate-hued sky
A maiden fair traipses through the thicket in her mind
Relentless beauty she sees all around her
Wondrous and winding be this haven of hers
Life abundant everywhere she turns
But still she moves as if in a trance
Depleted, afraid, alone, and lonely
No expression mars porcelain face
No trace of sadness, no sign of fear
For in the midst of this pain that pulses within her
An enduring flame deep inside her burns ever on
A glimmer of joy blinks behind her eyes
And this heaven through which she treads
Near the ocean, neighboring shore
A mirage of the oasis her soul cries out for
A wish, a desire that begs to be fulfilled
She dreams of raising her voice to the sky
Singing of love and joy, pain and sorrow
She wishes her words to infiltrate open hearts
To nevermore wander aimlessly
To find the purpose for it all

Dowry

I come to you empty-handed
Broke, and broken
The world I cannot gift you
Nor any treasure found thereon
I will make to you no promises
For I am human, and they may break
I've nothing but my damaged self to offer
Only my love to give
It is that love which holds me together
Keeps all of my shards and splinters joined
A mosaic of many wounds
Ever-present, though weather-beaten

This love is strength in its endurance
It is forgiveness, as it does not abandon at censure
It is courage in the face of rejection and hopelessness
It is kindness for its wanting of your truest happiness
Even if the source is not this love itself

It is honesty for its admission of its faults and many flaws
It is selflessness for the sacrifices it would make to see you thrive
It is pride in the glow of your numerous attributes
It is comfort, as it will always offer a home to rest your cares
It is perseverance, as it will never leave you to fight a battle alone
It is ambition for its boundless hope for fruition and reciprocation
It is intelligence for its knowledge of what will always and never be
It is boldness in its shameless display
It is prudence in its quiet adoration
It is this love, and all that it is
All that it gives to me
That I humbly bring to your table
As nourishment for your soul
You may opt to refuse or ignore
And in that event I will go

But my offer is never rescinded
Should you change your mind
My gift will be there still

Patchwork Dolls

To be broken from birth
Tangled shreds from the start
Never knowing what it's like
For the pieces to fit together
Spat out on cold floor
Left alone in the mess
To gather and puzzle yourself
Into something of use
For this world makes it clear
In scraping terms
That use defines purpose
And purpose defines worth
They look down their nose
At this pile of their making
And sneer with contempt
To deny their own blame
So you shoulder the guilt
Of your very existence
Which you couldn't have concocted
And don't know why you still choose it
The weight of these burdens
Has pinned down your wings
And obscured the reflection
Of your potential in the mirror
All these things I do see
And I'll not look away
These things I understand
Recognize my own plight
And for where our pieces fit
Jagged still, but holding firm
Hope we might yet find

The Counter Spell

Hanging low from familiar perch
Filigree cage dulled with rust
Ambivalent hues, indifferent grey
All the same since time began
No life outside is in the offing
I am fated to die where born
Swinging slow from suspended bar
No songs to pass the time
This bird fell silent long ago
Luting melodies strangled
By bellowing captor
Look yet again upon littered floor
A tiny winking pierces the blur
Odd, as surely nothing's changed
Flutter down to peck the crust
Chip away at the years of grime
And there it shone as blessed beacon
Emblazoned in discovery
A key, so small, of purest gold
Waiting patiently beneath the door
Incredulous
It was here all along
The beast weaved the cage
Tossed her in without care
But never had he held the key
That power was only bestowed upon her
To uncover in her own time
Blind she had become
From the horrors she had seen
Had been so certain
There was no life than this
Yet now her tears washed clean the dark
And she sang to the heavens in mighty release

The pall splintered and crumbled
To reveal sparkling skies
Limitless horizons awaiting her flight
Trembling, she launched with unfettered abandon
Swooping and soaring in heady delight
And there she stayed, unweighted
Imprisoned no longer
Endorsed herself to wield power
Allowed herself to fly free

Evergreen

Even that which falls misused
Need not die upon errant blade
Love doth wilt if cruelty starves
Yet can bloom anew with droplets shared

Crumble not your thirsting leaves
Though brittle they may be
Allow the rain to cleanse and quench
Revel in the life it revives

For true, each precious flora
At its roots, buried deep
Knows itself to be worthy
Its beauty and purpose inherent

Thus, it seeks the sun through darkness
Obscured, but only for a time
Dawn will emerge even surer than death
And fragile petals will again know warmth

And in time, often less than one might dream
Bright hues will newly grace their crowns
Heady aromas, dancing smoke upon the breeze
Dizzying in their glory, swaying in sweetness

The scent of life a'flourish
A cascade of colors bursting
From stems and trunks stronger than any storm
Their boughs embracing skies
And nary an eye that's worth its vision
Shall mistake this gorgeous rebirth
They will stare in awe, with tears a'sparkle
At your wondrous majesty that never was lost

Enlighten

Go forth into the twilight
Go beyond the skies
And see the visceral truth
In the depths of others' eyes
See the beautiful oddities
The differences you find
Speak silently with their spirits
Connect with their shrouded minds
For life is but a canvas
Brush strokes on the surface
An array of colors that give it breath
Never meant to be perfect

Worlds Asunder, Part III: Catharsis

When finally they parted, he cleaned her with reverence
Then she did same for him, to seal fond remembrance
They donned their robes, and she stepped toward the door
But he blocked her passage. "You'll not be his whore.
I can't make you a queen, but he'll do you far worse.
I'll go home alone to deal with his curse."
She pressed tearful face into ebony silk
"How will I know if he's done you ill?"
"If the moon blocks the sun so that day becomes night,
Just know I adore you and I've made his wrongs right."
A final kiss, whispered words, and he rode back to Hell
With the prayers of his angel keeping him well
Three more days' time and he patted his steed
Brushed her coat smooth and fine, and an extra bag of feed
"This might be it, Jezzy. I hope not, but we'll see.
If they don't treat you well, kick 'em harder for me."
He strode to the throne room, the gremlins jeering
They could smell her still on him, set them to leering
He entered with triumph, and his father was pleased
"I heard her screams down here, lad! Well done! Where's my queen?"
The son stood in silence, stance firm, chin high
"You'll have to kill me for her. She is well and wholly mine."
The Elder's grin fell as he accepted the dare
His advantage in all things was that he simply didn't care
"I understand your zeal, boy, but do not play the fool.
What would a princess expect to get from a failure like you?"
Never before had harpies' shrieks been so thoroughly drowned by swords
And when blades had broken, they bled new red into the molten floor
But mortal wound did find the son as father laid him low

The sun and moon rose darkly together, with an angel screaming "No!"

She dawned her shining armor then and raced to Hell below
Halting horse in king's great hall, she bellowed "Bring him to me NOW!"

"Ah, there's my queen, the saucy wench. Come, pet, you are now home."

"You've robbed me of my one true king. We both shall die alone!"

And raising blinding bow and string, her arrows God's own light

She made short work of all therein, and set the wrongs aright
But once they all had fallen, she knelt beside her love
Cradled his battered head in her lap, and kissed him over and over

She carried him then to the king's dark throne, and set him there to stay
And she seated herself in the queen's neighboring chair
His blood drying on her face

Surveying the room with its stench of gore, she held his lifeless hand

"Just know I adore you," and she ripped open her throat,

And the moon rose alone as the earth caved in.

Afterword

The human capacity for callousness is often devastating. Society at large considers it reprehensible for a person who has experienced abuse or mistreatment to speak out in anger against their tormentor(s). To do so sullies names, creates "problems", or opens "unnecessary" wounds. The concern and support most often given are overwhelmingly gifted to the abuser via absolutions such as these:

"You're too young to know what you're accusing them of. You just don't understand."

"There's no way they could have done what you're saying they did. I know them, better than you do, obviously."

"They're just not that type of person."

"You must have misinterpreted them."

"You're lying; I don't believe you."

"If they did it, they didn't mean to, or you deserved it."

"They have problems that they can't help. They just express themselves differently."

"They don't even remember doing it. Maybe you imagined it. Maybe you're crazy."

"That was just their bad side. They're not like that most of the time."

"You're the only one they've done this to. You must be the problem."

"What they did wasn't really that bad. Other people have been through much worse."

"If it never got physical, then it wasn't abuse."

"If it only happened once, then it wasn't abuse."

"This happened years ago; why dredge it up now?"

"You didn't speak up or leave soon enough; you've thrown away your chance."

"Move on already. You should be over this by now"

"Don't make their life harder just so you can feel better."

"You will only heal if you learn to forgive them."

"They said they were sorry; isn't that enough?"

"They were young at the time, didn't realize what they were doing."

"They're not the same person they used to be."

"Everyone makes mistakes. Give them a break."

"That's just how they are; let it roll off."

"They're a good person underneath. Just give them another chance."

"It was the drugs/alcohol; they just need rehab."

"They were raised that way; they can't help it."

"They obviously just need help. You should've been more supportive."

"If you had cared more about their wants/needs, you wouldn't be in this position."

"If you're going to call them out for every little mistake, then you're the one who's toxic."

"I don't want this getting out. It makes me uncomfortable, and might upset someone."

"If someone recognizes this person, then they'll recognize my connection to them, and then I'll be on display when I've done nothing wrong."

"What about their privacy? What about my privacy? Why can't you just keep it to yourself?"

"What is everyone going to think? What is everyone going to say?"

"How could you do this to my relative/friend/family/etc.? You've ruined them/us. You're so selfish."

"If they get wind of this, they might retaliate against you, or even me."

"Don't invite more trouble. Maybe you asked for it all along."

"Don't be surprised if they come after you. Everyone has the right to defend themselves. You just didn't do it well enough in the moment, so you've only yourself to blame."

"They could lose their family/friends/job over this. So could you. Why risk that by putting this out there?"

"The whole world doesn't need to know about this. You just want attention."

"You shouldn't have to be vocal about it to heal. Just keep it to yourself."

"You shouldn't have let yourself go. They wouldn't have done it if you were still attractive."

"There's no visible/physical evidence, so you have no credibility."

These examples are just the ones I've personally experienced or witnessed flung at others. Ultimately some people will say absolutely anything, even things that are clearly delusion or denial, to avoid accepting the damage that was done. It is all of these things and more that enable and empower an abuser. They depend on that, will manipulate, and incite it if they feel the need. This is why so many victims choose suffering in silence over reaching out in any way, sometimes literally dying in the process. It becomes an abhorrent scenario in which the victim fears public backlash even more than they fear the person inflicting the direct abuse. They've become somewhat numb and accustomed to the direct abuse, and that makes the lack of support from outsiders cut even deeper. That lack of support, that overt opposition to and denial of their reality, that defiant hostility reinforces that abuse, however indirect or unintentional. It only serves to invalidate the victim, which in turn validates the abuser. These attitudes are absorbed from the abuser and the culture that caters to them, and are then regurgitated out of desperation and fear. This imparts intimidation onto successive generations, thus allowing the cycle to continue. *That* is what sullies names. *That* is what creates problems and opens unnecessary wounds, for everyone involved. Evil breeds evil.

No one wants to accept or believe that someone they care for, are close to, or that they themselves could deliberately or repeatedly perpetuate such damage on another person, or on themselves. It can be equally traumatizing to witness as it is to receive. It is human instinct to preserve what good might yet remain among the bad, to protect and defend oneself and one's loved ones, even in the face of wrong-doing. An abuser hinges on this, uses it to successfully avoid accountability and retribution.

Even knowing all this, and seething with rage and despair from the injustice and audacity of it all, I still withhold names. I forego acknowledgements and dedications, just in case. I reword lines and omit stanzas. I blur details within concepts and distract with shocking fantasies. I omit some pieces entirely. Some experiences I have refused to even write about thus far. I anticipate some readers might recognize and make connections, might be appalled and repelled, might ask questions and issue rebuke, might attack or abandon me altogether - and I am stymied by fears and doubts. I am still afraid despite my boldness. I am resentful of my cowardice. I am still trapped within my release.

Only by affirming what we deny can we heal what festers, dispel the cloud-cover, and move forward to clear horizons. It is for all of these reasons that I rebel against absolute silence. Even in relative hiding I will rattle the cage bars. I will scream to the rafters from beneath my shield, if only to let go of what little I can. This burden's long been too heavy, and it's my turn to fly. For every wounded, caged creature that longs for freedom, know this: No bird ever has to earn their wings; they must only learn how to use them. No one should have to earn living life by their truth, or to dim their brightest star. Be a blaze in the darkness.

www.ingramcontent.com/pod-product-compliance
Lightning Source LLC
Chambersburg PA
CBHW051708040426
42446CB00008B/782